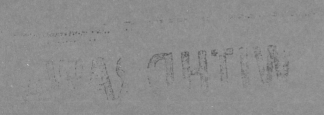

ALLIGATORS and CROCODILES

by GAIL GIBBONS

Holiday House / New York

To Doris Hipsher

*Special thanks to Bill Holmstrom,
herpetologist at the Bronx Zoo,
Bronx, New York, for reviewing
the text*

Copyright © 2010 by Gail Gibbons
All Rights Reserved
HOLIDAY HOUSE is registered in the U.S. Patent and Trademark Office.
Printed and bound January 2010 at Kwong Fat Offset Printing Co., Ltd.,
Dongguan City, Quangdong Province, China.
www.holidayhouse.com   First Edition   1 3 5 7 9 10 8 6 4 2
Library of Congress Cataloging-in-Publication Data
Gibbons, Gail.
Alligators and crocodiles / by Gail Gibbons. — 1st ed.
p. cm.
ISBN 978-0-8234-2234-0 (hardcover)
1. Alligators—Juvenile literature. 2. Crocodiles—Juvenile literature. I. Title.
QL666.C925G53 2010   597.980973—dc22   2009030293

Something glides slowly through the water, barely making a ripple. It is well hidden and looks like a bumpy drifting log. Two eyes and a snout appear above the water. It is an alligator or a crocodile.

ALLIGATOR

CROCODILE

All reptiles are cold-blooded animals. In order to survive, they must keep their body temperature from getting too hot or too cold. They do this by moving to a cooler or a warmer place.

Alligators and crocodiles are members of a group of reptiles called crocodilians (krok·uh·DILL·ee·ans). They are the closest living relatives of dinosaurs and the world's largest reptiles.

PALEONTOLOGISTS are scientists who learn about ancient life by studying fossils, the remains of a plant or animal that lived at least ten thousand years ago.

EXTINCT means no longer in existence.

According to paleontologists (pay·lee·on·TOL·o·jists), alligators, crocodiles, and dinosaurs lived on Earth about 230 million years ago. About 65 million years ago dinosaurs became extinct, but alligators and crocodiles continued to live.

Greek travelers saw crocodiles for the first time in Egypt.

The word "crocodile" comes from the word *krokodeilos*, (kro·KO·day·los), which means "lizard" in Greek.

Spanish soldiers saw alligators for the first time in North America.

The word "alligator" comes from *el lagarto* (L la·GAR·toe), which means "the lizard" in Spanish.

WHERE ALLIGATORS AND CROCODILES LIVE

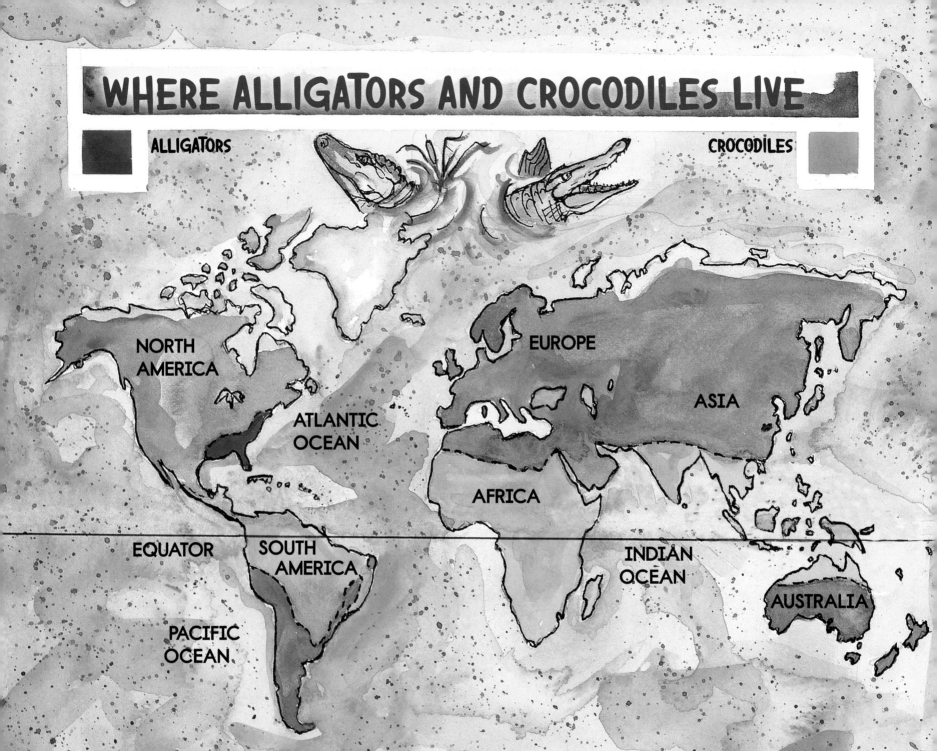

ALLIGATORS

CROCODILES

NORTH AMERICA

EUROPE

ASIA

ATLANTIC OCEAN

AFRICA

EQUATOR

SOUTH AMERICA

INDIAN OCEAN

AUSTRALIA

PACIFIC OCEAN

There are two different kinds of alligators and fourteen different kinds of crocodiles. The only area inhabited by both alligators and crocodiles is the southern tip of Florida and the Florida Keys.

WHERE AMERICAN ALLIGATORS AND CROCODILES LIVE IN THE UNITED STATES

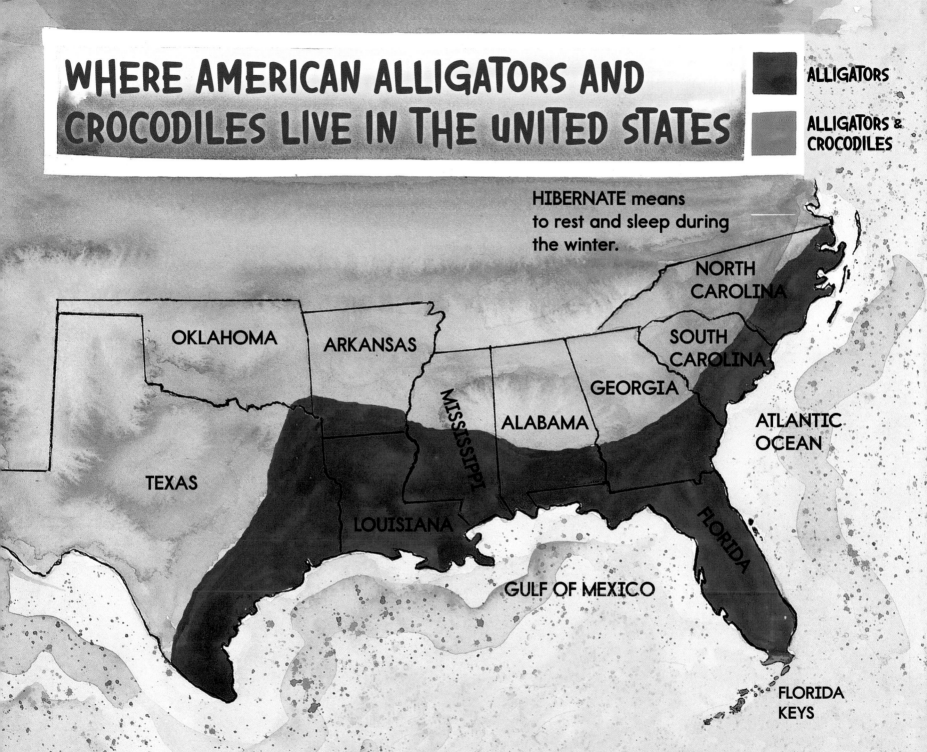

ALLIGATORS

ALLIGATORS & CROCODILES

HIBERNATE means to rest and sleep during the winter.

NORTH CAROLINA

SOUTH CAROLINA

OKLAHOMA

ARKANSAS

GEORGIA

MISSISSIPPI

ALABAMA

ATLANTIC OCEAN

TEXAS

LOUISIANA

FLORIDA

GULF OF MEXICO

FLORIDA KEYS

Alligators and crocodiles usually live in climates where the water and air temperatures are warm all year long. Some alligators live in cooler climates where they must hibernate if it gets too cold.

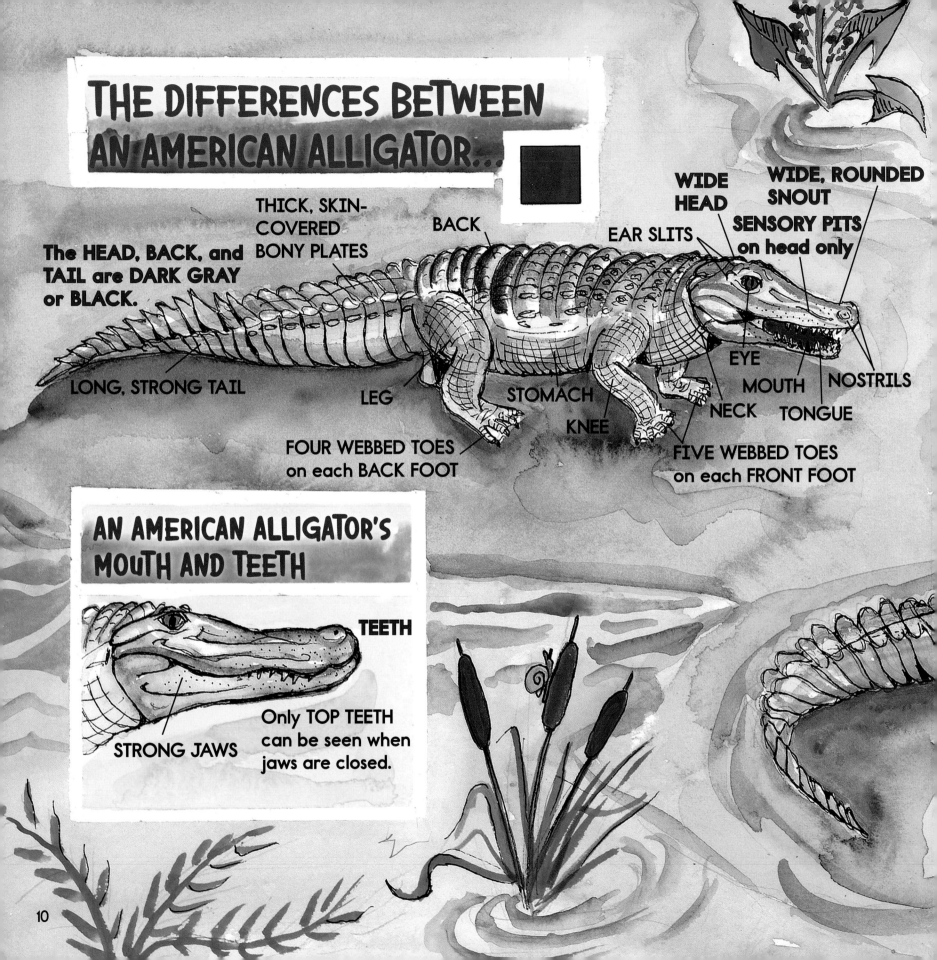

THE DIFFERENCES BETWEEN AN AMERICAN ALLIGATOR...

WIDE HEAD

WIDE, ROUNDED SNOUT

SENSORY PITS on head only

EAR SLITS

BACK

THICK, SKIN-COVERED BONY PLATES

The HEAD, BACK, and TAIL are DARK GRAY or BLACK.

EYE

MOUTH

NOSTRILS

NECK

TONGUE

LONG, STRONG TAIL

LEG

STOMACH

KNEE

FOUR WEBBED TOES on each BACK FOOT

FIVE WEBBED TOES on each FRONT FOOT

AN AMERICAN ALLIGATOR'S MOUTH AND TEETH

TEETH

STRONG JAWS

Only TOP TEETH can be seen when jaws are closed.

10

AND AN AMERICAN CROCODILE

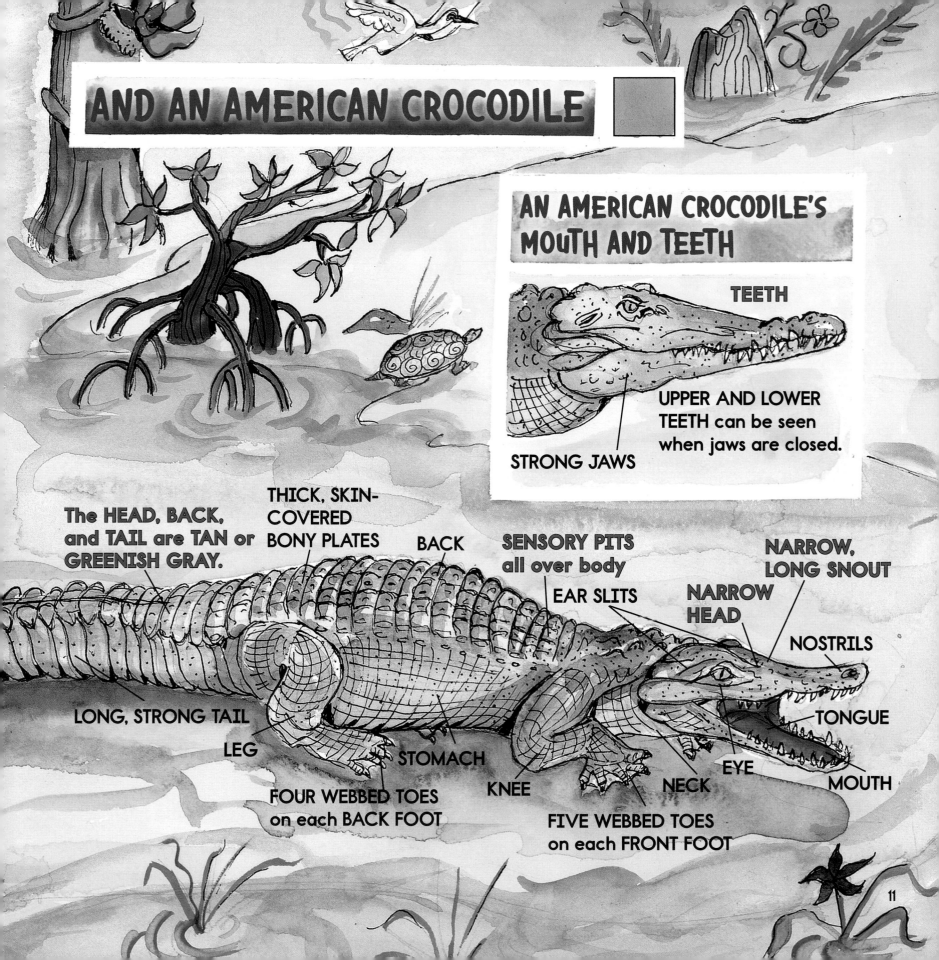

AN AMERICAN CROCODILE'S MOUTH AND TEETH

TEETH

STRONG JAWS

UPPER AND LOWER TEETH can be seen when jaws are closed.

The HEAD, BACK, and TAIL are TAN or GREENISH GRAY.

THICK, SKIN-COVERED BONY PLATES

BACK

SENSORY PITS all over body

EAR SLITS

NARROW HEAD

NARROW, LONG SNOUT

NOSTRILS

LONG, STRONG TAIL

LEG

STOMACH

KNEE

NECK

EYE

TONGUE

MOUTH

FOUR WEBBED TOES on each BACK FOOT

FIVE WEBBED TOES on each FRONT FOOT

Alligators and crocodiles each have about sixty pointed teeth.

When they lose a tooth, a new tooth takes its place.

CARNIVORES are animals that eat meat.

They can grow about three thousand new teeth during their lives.

Alligators and crocodiles are carnivores. To catch their prey, they may stay perfectly still. When an animal comes near . . . SNAP! The animal is grabbed in a split second. Alligators and crocodiles may also swim slowly and quietly to their unaware prey and attack.

Cold-blooded animals do not eat as often as warm-blooded animals.

Young alligators and crocodiles usually feed on small prey such as fish, frogs, and birds, using their powerful jaws and sharp teeth. Larger, older alligators and crocodiles may eat big animals such as raccoons and deer. Often they grab their prey and hold its nose underwater until the animal drowns. Also, they may leap to catch their prey. They eat by ripping the animal apart and swallowing the pieces whole.

ALLIGATORS AND CROCODILES LIVE IN THE WATER...

They can swim up to 6 miles (9.6 kilometers) an hour.

Alligators and crocodiles are good swimmers and spend most of their time in the water. They use their powerful, swishing tails to move forward.

They can stay underwater
for as long as two hours.

They are able to steer using their tails and back legs. By tucking in
all four legs they are able to swim faster.

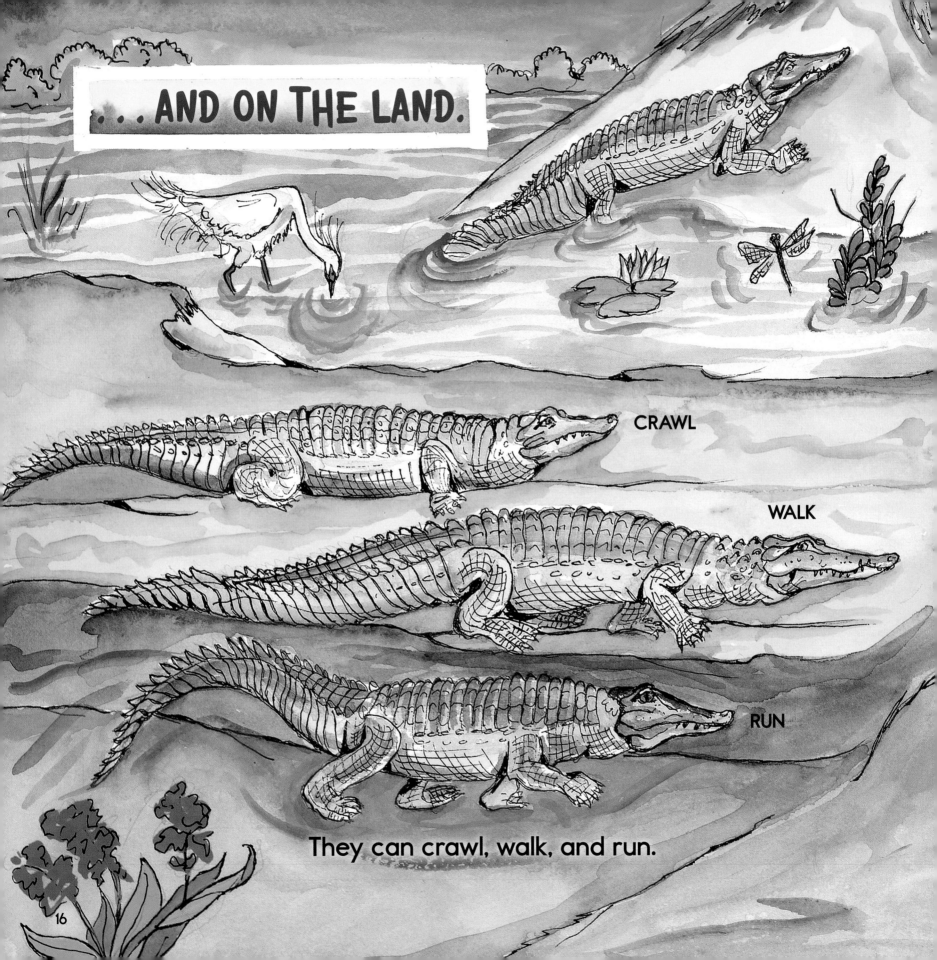

... AND ON THE LAND.

CRAWL

WALK

RUN

They can crawl, walk, and run.

HIGH WALK

Sometimes they walk with their bodies high off the ground. This is called the "high walk."

NOCTURNAL means
being active at night.

Alligators and crocodiles are nocturnal. They see well in the dark.
They also see far away very well. They cannot see well underwater.

The SHALLOW NERVES are under the skin on top of their heads.

Each EAR is hidden behind a slit in the skin.

Crocodiles and alligators have excellent senses of smell. They also have excellent senses of hearing. They are able to pick up vibrations in the air or water, using their ears as well as the shallow nerves on top of their heads.

Sensory pits on their bodies also help detect vibrations in the water. Vibrations alert them to any nearby prey. The thick, bony plates of American alligators and American crocodiles help protect them.

Alligators and crocodiles can make roaring, grumbling, and hissing sounds when they are protecting their territory. They will puff out their necks to show that they are ready to fight.

During mating season, males and females communicate by making grunts, barks, and low, rumbling sounds. Often they rub snouts, blow bubbles on the water's surface, and swim together in circles. Sometimes they will make sounds by slapping the surface of the water to attract a mate. They mate underwater.

AN AMERICAN ALLIGATOR'S NEST

The female lays about forty-five eggs on a bed of leaves and grasses. She then completely covers them with a mound made of leaves, grasses, and mud. The mound is about 6 feet (1.8 meters) wide.

MOUND

NEST

EGGS

AN AMERICAN CROCODILE'S NEST

The female digs a hole in the ground and lays about fifty eggs. She covers each layer and the top with sand.

NEST

EGGS

A group of eggs is called a CLUTCH.

A few weeks later the females lay their eggs in nests, where the eggs will be kept warm and protected. Mother alligators and crocodiles are always on the alert, guarding their nests to protect their young from any egg-eating animals, such as skunks and raccoons.

The warmth of the inside of the nest helps determine whether the newborns will be males or females. When the temperature of the nest is above 88° Fahrenheit (31° Celsius), most of the hatchlings will be males. When the temperature is lower, most will be females.

AMERICAN ALLIGATOR

The mother can hear her young making squeaking sounds from inside the eggs. They are ready to hatch.

Sometimes the mother uses her tongue to roll an egg against the roof of her mouth. Soon the shell cracks open and the hatchling crawls out.

A baby may use its EGG TOOTH to crack open the hard shell and break free.

AMERICAN ALLIGATOR HATCHLING

Usually it takes about sixty-five days before the allligator and crocodile eggs begin to hatch. Newborns are called hatchlings.

Most hatchlings are about 10 inches (25.4 centimeters) long. Within minutes of hatching, their mother takes them to the water.

An American crocodile can grow to be about 20 feet (6 meters) long.

An American alligator can grow to be about 12 feet (3.6 meters) long.

The hatchlings have needle-sharp teeth and can hunt and feed on small fish and insects right away.

American alligator hatchlings have yellow stripes on their bodies, which fade away as they grow older.

The female alligator and crocodile stay close to their young for about a year. They protect them from harm before the young ones go off on their own. Young alligators and crocodiles grow about 1 foot (.3 meter) a year for their first six years. As they get older, they grow slower. They continue to grow throughout their lives.

Alligators and crocodiles use their strong legs, feet, and tails to dig holes in muddy marshlands. The holes fill with water. Other wildlife living nearby will also make use of these water holes.

American alligators and American crocodiles were hunted for hundreds of years for their meat and skins. Today it is illegal to hunt them, but humans are still their main enemy.

People have developed areas where these large reptiles once lived. There are fewer and fewer places where alligators and crocodiles can live in their natural environment.

Wildlife preserves have been created to protect them.

ENDANGERED means
threatened with
extinction.

Alligators and crocodiles have been around for millions of years.
Now they are endangered. The lives of these fascinating creatures
should be respected.

MORE ABOUT ALLIGATORS AND CROCODILES...

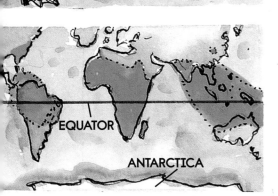

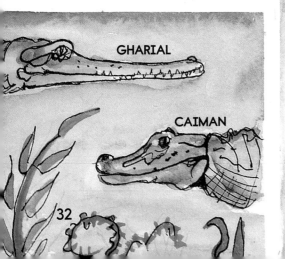

GHARIAL

CAIMAN

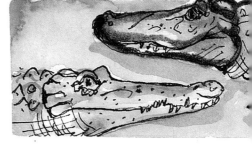

LA

Some ancient Egyptians worshipped Sobek, a god whose head was shaped like that of a crocodile.

A crocodile can slam down its jaws using about 13 tons (11.8 metric tons) of pressure!

Crocodilians live on all the continents except Antarctica and Europe.

In addition to alligators and crocodiles, there are two other members of the crocodilian family. Gharials (GARE·ee·uls) are found in India and southest Asia. Caimans (KAY·muns) are found in Central America and South America.

Scientists believe that alligators and crocodiles can live to be about seventy years old in the wild.

A group of young hatchlings is called a crèche (KRESH).

The largest American alligator ever found in the wild was about 19 feet (5.8 meters) long. It was found in 1890 in Louisiana.

After a large meal, it is possible for an adult alligator or crocodile to go for many months without having to eat again.

To learn more about crocodilians visit www.crocodilian.com

EQUATOR

ANTARCTICA

32